Kipper
Kipper's Toybox
Kipper's Birthday
Kipper and Roly
Kipper's Monster
Kipper's Beach Ball
Kipper's Snowy Day
Kipper's Christmas Eve
Hide Me, Kipper!

Kipper Storyboards:
Playtime!
Miaow!
Castle
Swing!
Honk!
Hisssss!
Butterfly
Splosh!

First Kipper:
Colours
Counting
Opposites
Weather

Kipper's A to Z
One Year with Kipper
Kipper Story Collection

First published in 2002
by Hodder Children's Books

This edition published in 2008

Text and illustrations copyright © Mick Inkpen 2002

Hodder Children's Books
338 Euston Road
London NW1 3BH

Hodder Children's Books Australia
Level 17/207 Kent Street
Sydney, NSW 2000

The right of Mick Inkpen to be identified as the
author and the illustrator of this Work has been
asserted by him in accordance with the Copyright,
Designs and Patents Act 1988.

ISBN: 978 0 340 93208 7
10 9 8 7 6 5

Printed in China

Hodder Children's Books is a division of
Hachette Children's Books.
An Hachette UK Company.
www.hachette.co.uk

What any author wants is for his books to become dog-eared and familiar. I've been lucky enough that my very young readers are particularly adept at giving their books doggy ears in no time at all.

And of all my books, perhaps it's those about Kipper that get the doggiest ears of all, which I guess is kind of appropriate.

Mick Inkpen

Kipper's Monster
Mick Inkpen

Hodder
Children's
Books

A division of Hachette Children's Books

Tiger had a brand new torch.
'It's the most powerful torch
there is!' he said to Kipper.
He shone it at Big Owl.
He shone it at Hippo.
He shone it in Kipper's face.
'You should see it when it's
dark!' he said. 'It's REALLY good
when it's dark!'

He sat in Kipper's basket and pulled the blanket over his head.

'Come on! We can make it dark under here!' he said.

Under the blanket was one of Kipper's storybooks.

'That's another thing!' said Tiger. 'You can read under the bedclothes with a torch like this!'

Kipper began to read.
'Deep in the middle of the
dark, dark wood, there lived a horrible,
horrendous, terrible, tremendous…'

'That's it!' shouted Tiger, jumping up.
'We'll camp in the woods tonight!
It'll be really, REALLY dark in
the woods.'

'Shall I bring my
book?' said Kipper.

So they took the book and some biscuits and they put up their tent in the middle of the woods, at the bottom of Big Hill.

But as it began to get dark Tiger began to think that perhaps it wasn't such a good idea after all.

'Come inside and have a biscuit,' said Kipper. 'Do you want Rabbit or Big Owl?'

But Tiger didn't reply. He was looking nervously out of the door. 'Do you think there are any bears in these woods?' he whispered.

'No, I shouldn't think so,' said Kipper. He began to read.

'Deep in the middle of the dark, dark wood, there lived a horrible…'

But Tiger wasn't ready. He asked Kipper to sit next to the door, instead of him. And when Kipper tried again to read, Tiger got up and zipped the door shut altogether.

B ut the third time Kipper tried
to read, from somewhere
outside the tent, there came the
most terrible, tremendous, horrible,
horrendous,

'Screech!'

'What was that?' said Kipper. Tiger said nothing.

'Let's go and look!' whispered Kipper. So they crept out of the tent and into the woods, shining Tiger's torch ahead of them.

'I think it came from somewhere near here,' said Kipper. The torch beam lit up the enormous, grey trunk of an old tree.

There in the middle was a dark, dark hole.

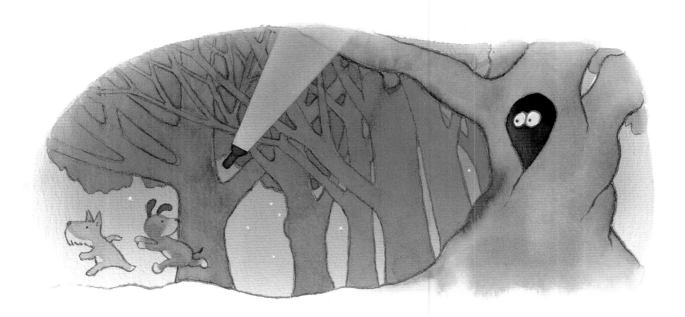

S uddenly a huge pair of
yellow eyes blinked open, and
from the hole came the most terrible,

'Screech!'

They shrieked and ran, bumping
into each other and sending the
torch flying. They scrambled into the
tent and lay there panting hard,
listening…

'I think it was just an owl,' whispered Kipper. 'Yes, it was just a silly, old owl.'

But behind him, the shadow of something was growing on the wall of the tent.

Something with horns.

'It's a horrible, horrendous monster!' squealed Tiger. The shape on the tent grew and grew till it was looming above them. Then it slowly changed into a shape that Kipper had seen before.

Kipper crept back out of the tent and walked towards the torchlight. There, caught in the beam, was a little snail.

Kipper picked up the torch and let the snail crawl on to his paw. He looked at the snail closely.

Its horns curled in and out as he touched them.

'I've found the horrible, horrendous monster! Look Tiger!'

Tiger peeped out from underneath the blanket.

He saw the snail.

He saw its shadow.

He felt silly.

'Shall I read the story now?'
said Kipper.

But Kipper never did get to read his story, because they went home to Tiger's house, where they put up the tent in Tiger's bedroom…

…and Tiger got to read it instead.

'My children absolutely LOVE all of Mick Inkpen's books, and I still love reading Kipper to them, even when it's for the hundredth time...'

CRESSIDA COWELL

'He is the perfect pup to grow up with...'

HILARY MCKAY